Dying to
Live

James A. Harnish

Dying to Live

A LENTEN STUDY FOR ADULTS

Abingdon Press / Nashville

DYING TO LIVE
A LENTEN STUDY FOR ADULTS

Copyright © 2003 by Abingdon Press.

All rights reserved.

This book is printed on acid-free, elemental chlorine-free paper.

Library of Congress Cataloging-in-Publication Data

Harnish, James A.
    Dying to live : a Lenten study for adults / James A. Harnish.
        p. cm.
    ISBN 0-687-06336-1 (alk. paper)
    1. Lent—Meditations.   I. Title.

BV85 .H345 2002
242' .34—dc21

2002153409

Scripture quotations, unless otherwise noted, are from the New Revised Standard Version of the Bible, copyright © 1989, by the Division of Christian Education of the National Council of the Churches of Christ in the United States of America. Used by permission.

Scripture quotations marked *Message* are taken from THE MESSAGE. Copyright © Eugene H. Peterson, 1993, 1994, 1995. Used by permission of NavPress Publishing Group.

03 04 05 06 07 08 09 10 11 12 — 10 9 8 7 6 5 4 3 2 1

"Our firm decision is to work from this focused center: One man died for everyone. That puts every-one in the same boat. He included everyone in his death so that everyone could also be included in his life, a resurrection life, a far better life than people ever lived on their own."

2 Corinthians 5:14-15, *Message*

Contents

Introduction

Dying to Live
Answers to the Question,
Why Did Jesus Die on the Cross?

When historian Stephen Ambrose told the downright amazing story of the building of the transcontinental railroad that linked Chicago and San Francisco, he titled his book *Nothing Like It in the World* (Simon & Schuster, 2000). He compared the construction of the railroad to the Civil War, in which many of the railroad's builders had just fought.

> There was but one single decisive spot. The builders could not outflank an enemy, or attack in an unexpected place, or encircle. The end of the track, the place where the rails gave out, was the only spot that mattered. Only there could the line advance, only there could the battle be joined.

During the forty days of Lent, we are invited to take a spiritual journey to the single, decisive spot in human history where the ultimate battle of good and evil was joined. The Gospel writers are clear that there was no way for Jesus to outflank or avoid it. The inevitable end of the track he followed, the only spot that ultimately mattered, was a cross. And there really has never been anything like it in the world.

The pivotal event upon which the whole Christian tradition hangs is that on a particular Friday afternoon, around A.D. 33, Jesus of Nazareth died as a convicted felon on a Roman cross outside the city of Jerusalem; and then three days later he was raised from the dead. Professor S. Mark Heim declares that Christ's death on the cross is "so integral to the grammar of faith that its absence amounts to a debilitating speech defect. A church that falls silent about the cross has a hole where the gospel ought to be" ("Christ Crucified," *The Christian Century*, March 7, 2001, page 12).

Most people would agree that the cross is central to the Christian faith, but that doesn't mean we understand it. There is great mystery here. I suspect that one of the reasons it has been the subject of so much of the world's great art and music is that the event itself, along with its impact on human history, staggers our comprehension and goes deeper than easy explanation. If we tell the truth, Jesus' death on the cross raises mind-bending, soul-stretching questions for everyone who searches for a meaningful faith.

Why did Jesus die on the cross?

What did his death accomplish?

What real difference does the cross make in our lives, our world, and our relationship with God?

As the early Christians struggled to define their identity in a pagan and often hostile world, they were forced to answer challenging questions about the crucifixion of Jesus. The first Christian sermon, preached by Peter on the Day of Pentecost, was an attempt to interpret the meaning of the cross and the Resurrection to Jewish pilgrims in Jerusalem (Acts 2:14-39). Stephen proclaimed the same interpretation of the death and resurrection of Jesus prior to becoming the first martyr for the faith (Acts 7). From the very beginning of the Christian movement, the bold claim that God had raised the crucified Messiah demanded both explanation and application. Following these examples in the Book of Acts, Christian people have been working on that task ever since.

When theologians study the cross, they use the word *atonement*. It literally means "to make at one," or "at-*one*-ment." Christian believers claim that the cross is God's action to set right the "gone-wrong-ness" of human life (*Interpretation*, January 1998; page 4), to heal the estrangement in our relationships with God and with one another, and to restore wholeness to this sin-damaged creation.

In searching for the best way to explain their faith, the New Testament writers engaged a wide variety of traditions and images from the Old Testament and from the culture around them. As we make our way toward the cross in this study, we will look at several of the classic "theories of the atonement," not for the purpose of scholarly analysis, but to experience the impact of God's action at the cross in our own lives. The questions at the end of each chapter are designed to serve as the outline for small-group discussion or as a guide for persons engaged in personal reflection or spiritual journaling.

My prayer is that as we share this journey to the "single decisive spot" where the struggle of good and evil was joined, we will discover God's power to transform our lives. In the language of Ambrose, there is no way to outflank or avoid it. The only place that really matters is the place where the track ran out for Jesus' earthly life. The only place that matters is the cross. And there's nothing like it in the world!

Why Did Jesus Die on the Cross? To Show the Way: Living a Cross-Shaped Life

1 Peter 2:21; Philippians 3:7-17

I don't even try to read all of the jokes, stories, advertisements, and "spam" messages that come my way over the Internet. People who have time to read all that stuff have too much time on their hands! I do, however, give priority to anything that comes from my daughters, one of whom sent me a list of "Life's Imponderables." They are questions for which there never seems to be a simple, clear, or adequate answer. Here are a few of them.

Why is *abbreviation* such a long word?
How do they get deer to cross the highway at the yellow signs?
How did a fool and his money get together in the first place?
What was the best thing *before* sliced bread?

One of my own imponderables comes out of my adolescence. You probably need to be part of the baby-boom generation to fully appreciate it. My question is, Why did the little records have the big holes, and the big records have the little holes? It's imponderable, but it really doesn't matter because no one plays vinyl records anymore!

Imponderable questions. Questions for which there seem to be no simple, complete, or adequate answers. This one really matters: Why did Jesus die on the cross?

One response to that question is known as the "moral influence" theory of atonement. Its roots go back to a twelfth-century theologian named Peter Abelard, who taught that the cross was history's greatest example of God's love. He believed that by seeing the beauty and power of God's love at the cross, people would be inspired to live according to the way of love that was modeled for us in Jesus. He believed that the cross could be a formative influence on human behavior. You could say that it was a twelfth-century version of the WWJD bracelets that were so popular a few years ago. Wearing the bracelet was a reminder to ask yourself, in any given situation, *What Would Jesus Do?* A key text for this perspective on the atonement is found in the First Epistle of Peter: "For to this you have been called, because Christ also suffered for you, leaving you an example, so that you should follow in his steps" (1 Peter 2:21).

William J. O'Malley is a teacher and writer on character and faith development in youth. He affirmed the character-shaping influence of the cross when he wrote, "Christianity is a crucifix: a man utterly used up for others. The true Christian looks at it and says, 'Yes. That's the most perfectly fulfilled human being who ever lived, caught at the moment of his greatest triumph. I want to be like him'" (*Context*, January 15, 2001; page 6).

Here's the key affirmation: Jesus died on the cross to show us the way to live. He gave his life to show us the way that leads to life—real life, abundant life, life the way God intends for it to be lived, life so alive that it can never be put to death. We are called to follow in his steps by living a cross-shaped life.

The moral influence of the cross moves beyond simple knowledge of a historical event to a subjective experience of the love of God that can make a practical difference in the way we live, act, and relate to others. It has a radical impact on the way we respond to violence, political power, and the complex social issues of our day. It changes our perspective on the way we use our resources, view the world around us, and look toward the future. We're talking about the love of God that was made real in the life, death, and resurrection of Jesus, becoming a tangible reality in each of our lives and in our life together. The church does not exist to recruit people as members, but to transform them into disciples of a crucified Lord. In that transformation process, the love of God revealed at the cross becomes the formative influence that shapes our life from the inside out.

That's what the gospel describes. That's what the New Testament promises. Perhaps the most imponderable thing is how easily we miss it.

When I get to heaven, I plan to ask God some tough questions. Here are a few of them:

How is it that people can sit on the same church pew week after week, listen to the Scripture, sing the hymns, go to a Sunday school class, and still be just as ornery, mean, and nasty as anyone else?

How is it that we can hear the story of the passion and death of Jesus year after year but end up being just as greedy, selfish, and self-absorbed as we would have been had we never heard the story at all?

How is it that people can read the Sermon on the Mount year in and year out and not hear Jesus' clear call to a life of nonviolence?

How can we see what God did on the cross and go on living the same old life in the same old way? Peter declared that Jesus suffered to leave us an example so that we might follow in his steps. Jesus died on the cross to show us how to live a cross-shaped life.

In his letter to the Philippians, the apostle Paul shared his spiritual autobiography, describing the difference Christ made in his life. He began by recounting all the things that were important in his life.

> If anyone else has reason to be confident in the flesh, I have more: circumcised on the eighth day, a member of the people of Israel, of the tribe of Benjamin, a Hebrew born of Hebrews; as to the law, a Pharisee; as to zeal, a persecutor of the church; as to righteousness under the law, blameless.   (Philippians 3:4-6)

Education, prestige, position, influence, authority: Paul had them all. But listen for the difference Christ made in his life.

Yet whatever gains I had, these I have come to regard as loss because of Christ. More than that, I regard everything as loss because of the surpassing value of knowing Christ Jesus my Lord. For his sake I have suffered the loss of all things, and I regard them as rubbish, in order that I may gain Christ and be found in him. . . . I want to know Christ and the power of his resurrection and the sharing of his sufferings by becoming like him in his death, if somehow I may attain the resurrection from the dead.

Not that I have already obtained this or have already reached the goal; but I press on to make it my own, because Christ Jesus has made me his own. (Philippians 3:7-12)

Talk about "moral influence"! The love of God in Christ had become the formative influence in Paul's attitudes, values, and relationships. He does not say that he wants to know *about* Christ, the way a person might collect interesting facts about a historical figure. He wants to *know* Christ, the way intimate friends know each other and share their life together. He wants the life of Jesus to be the determinative force in his personality. Paul points to three critical elements in the formation of a cross-shaped life.

First, a cross-shaped life shares Jesus' suffering.

Have you read *Tuesdays with Morrie*? Mitch Albom's diary of his weekly conversations with his dying college mentor has sold more than five million copies in thirty-one different languages. Morrie's words and the way he faced his death have touched a deep nerve in millions of lives. When Albom was interviewed in *Time* magazine, he said, "When Morrie was his weakest and his most helpless, that's when he had the most to offer" (*Time*, February 26, 2001; page G4).

The New Testament declares that when Jesus was his weakest, when he was the most helpless, when he was hanging naked and bleeding on the cross, he had the most to offer. In fact, it declares that by his powerless love, Jesus overcame all of the world's loveless power. We are promised that as we enter into his suffering we begin to experience the depth of the love and grace of God.

I sometimes wish it were the other way around. I wish he had

15

had the most to offer when he was at his greatest strength, because that's the way I'd like to be known. I'd like people to know me at my best, at my strongest, at the times and places where I appear to be the most capable and competent. But I've discovered that it just doesn't work that way. We don't really know one another until we are known in our weakness and vulnerability.

No wonder that Paul called the cross a scandal, an outrage, sheer foolishness to those in the world who are perishing (*see* 1 Corinthians 1:18). But he was convinced that "God's foolishness is wiser than human wisdom, and God's weakness is stronger than human strength" (1 Corinthians 1:25). In weakness we discover the power of God's love.

On a visit to The Riverside Church in New York, I once heard William Sloane Coffin say that the tragedy in life is not that we suffer. All of us suffer. The tragedy, he said, is suffering that never gets redeemed, suffering that never gets healed, suffering that never leads to greater strength, suffering that never leads to new life. Jesus died on the cross to meet us in our weakness, so that by his suffering our suffering might be made useful, might be redeemed.

Living a cross-shaped life also means sharing, as Jesus shared, the suffering of others. Followers of the cross are called to take into their own experience the suffering experienced by brothers and sisters in the human family. This is what Paul meant when he told the Colossian Christians, "I am now rejoicing in my suffering for your sake, and in my flesh I am completing what is lacking in Christ's afflictions" (Colossians 1:24).

The truth about my life—I suspect it is true for you, too!—is that I easily can ignore the pain and suffering of people around me. The world in which I live offers a multitude of distractions from the hurt that is inflicted on innocent people in a world that values loveless power infinitely more than it values powerless love. I don't have to work very hard to find socially acceptable ways to avoid the situations and relationships that remind me of the impact of poverty, injustice, prejudice, and oppression in the lives of people in my community and people around the world. I'm very capable of closing my eyes to the destruction that is inflicted on the lives of people in the Third World, because I live in a consumer culture. Were it not for the love of God revealed at the cross, I could easily protect myself from the massive suffering of our world.

But I am discovering that the closer I get to Jesus, the closer I get to the suffering of others. The more intentionally I attempt to live my life on the basis of his life, the more I find myself being drawn into the lives of others, to share their hurt, to know their pain, and to join them in their suffering. The amazing irony is that I also am discovering that the more fully I connect with the suffering of others, the more fully I understand the suffering of Jesus. The more intimately I share the sorrow other people feel, the more intimately I comprehend the sorrow that caused Jesus to weep by the grave of Lazarus (John 11:32-35) and the anguish that made him weep over the city of Jerusalem (Luke 19:41-42).

The second critical element that Paul pointed to in the formation of a cross-shaped life is this: A cross-shaped life involves becoming like Jesus in his death.

There are, of course, folks who on Good Friday pick up a cross and walk through the center of the city. There are even a few who dramatize having themselves nailed to a cross, though they never stay there very long. But that's not what it means to become like Jesus in his death. Paul is not saying that we should imitate crucifixion. He is saying that we should move through life toward our own death, the same way Jesus moved through his life toward his death. It is a call to face life with the same self-giving obedience and absolute trust in God as the obedience and trust with which Jesus faced his death.

I have news for you today: You are going to die. None of us will get out of this world alive. We deny it, we wrestle with it, we make bad jokes about it; but the truth is that all of us will die. The question is not, *Will* I die? The question is, *How* will I die? The question is not, Will I face the pain of death? The question is, What spiritual resources will I bring to my experience of dying? Will I have lived with God in such a way that I will have developed the same kind of trust in God that we see in Jesus when, with his dying breath, he said, "Father, into your hands I commend my spirit" (Luke 23:46)? Those words were a Hebrew child's prayer, like saying, "Now I lay me down to sleep." Through all of his suffering, Jesus was able to trust himself fully and freely into the goodness of God. The only way to be prepared to face death that way is to face life that way, to live with a growing trust in the goodness and greatness of God.

Becoming like Jesus in his death also means being willing to die to things that are less than the way and will of Jesus in our lives. Jesus called his disciples to take up their cross, deny themselves, and follow him in the way that led to the cross. Dietrich Bonhoeffer, whose theology was forged in the blast furnace of Nazi oppression, said that when Christ calls a person to be his disciple, he calls that person to come and die. "The cross is laid on every Christian. It begins with the call to abandon the attachments of this world. . . . As we embark upon discipleship we surrender ourselves to Christ in union with His death" (*The Cost of Discipleship*, New York: Macmillan, 1949; page 73).

If we are to be like Jesus, there will be old attitudes, old attachments, old values, and old prejudices within us that must go to the cross and die so that we can experience the new life he has to give. Like Jesus, we will die to the world's ideas of loveless power so that we can become the present expression of the powerless love that went to the cross. To be like Jesus in his death is to learn what the apostle meant when he said, "I have been crucified with Christ; and it is no longer I who live, but it is Christ who lives in me" (Galatians 2:19-20).

The third element that Paul pointed to as critical in the formation of a cross-shaped life is this: A cross-shaped life experiences the power of Jesus' resurrection.

I love the story of the preacher who was waxing eloquent on heaven and said to the congregation, "Everyone who wants to go to heaven, stand up!" They all stood up, all except old Joe in the back row. The preacher looked back at him and said, "Joe, don't you want to go to heaven when you die?" Joe replied, "Well, sure, when I die—but I thought you were getting up some folks to go right now!"

When Paul talked about knowing Christ in the power of his resurrection, he was talking about life after death, sure enough.

I rejoice in the hope of new life that will be fulfilled on the other side of death. But Paul was also talking about the power of the risen Christ at work in life right now. When he told the Galatians, "It is no longer I who live, but it is Christ who lives in me," he was describing how the power of God that raised Jesus from the dead can become the life-giving power in our present experience, energizing us and shaping our lives in the likeness of Christ. William Sloane Coffin proclaimed this truth in an Easter sermon when he said, "Christ is risen *pro nobis,* for us, to put love in our hearts, decent thoughts in our heads, and a little more iron up our spines. Christ is risen to convert us, not from life to something more than life, but from something less than life to the possibility of full life itself" ("Sermons from Riverside," April 3, 1983; page 3).

The liturgical tradition of setting aside the forty days of Lent for spiritual reflection and self-examination is patterned after the forty days Jesus spent in the wilderness (Matthew 4:1-11). But if you count the days from Ash Wednesday to Easter, you'll find more than forty days. That's because the forty days of Lent exclude Sundays, since Sunday is always the day of Resurrection; it is always the day upon which the church celebrates the living presence of the risen Christ, even when we are walking a path that leads to the cross.

To affirm that Christ is risen means that whenever we walk through the dark valley of the shadow of death, the risen Christ walks with us. The power of the Resurrection is available to energize us and to give us the present hope and joy of resurrection. A cross-shaped life is a life empowered by the presence of the risen Christ. This reality was captured in a simple Easter song that I remember teaching children several years ago. It said, "Every morning is Easter morning from now on." To experience the power of Jesus' resurrection is to live every day in the fullness of life that we find in the living presence of the risen Christ.

Each Lent I am drawn back to an old hymn that I remember singing as a teenager in the Methodist Youth Fellowship. It asks, " 'Are ye able,' said the Master, 'to be crucified with me?' " It's a tough question. The chorus replies, "Lord, we are able"!

19

Looking out at the very ordinary folks in my congregation and looking into the very ordinary corners of my own soul, I sometimes wonder if we should ever sing this hymn. Who among us would dare to declare, "Lord, we are able"? But the refrain goes on to say, "Our spirits are thine. Remold them, make us, like thee, divine." The bad news is that in our human power we are not able to live the cross-shaped life to which Jesus calls us. The good news is that the power of the risen Christ is available to remold us and make us into the likeness of Jesus. Jesus gave his life to show us the way to life; and in the Resurrection, he gives us power to live it!

Questions for Discussion and Reflection

1. Who or what have been the major influences in your life? How have they influenced your values, convictions, and perspective on the world?

2. What does it mean for you to ask, What would Jesus do? How does 1 Peter 2:21 speak to your experience? What practical difference does it make in your life to hear or read about the cross?

3. What's your experience with suffering? When have you been vulnerable to another person? How have you experienced God's presence in your weakness?

4. How do you face death? What would it mean for you to live with the kind of obedience and trust that Jesus demonstrated on the way to the cross?

5. How do you experience the power of the Resurrection in your daily life? What difference does it make for you to believe that Christ is risen in the present tense?

Prayer

O Loving God, give us grace to follow in the way of the cross until, by the influence of your Spirit, our lives are remade into the cross-shaped likeness of your Son, our Savior, Jesus Christ. Amen.

Second Week in Lent

Why Did Jesus Die on the Cross? To Redeem: What's God Doing Here?

Ephesians 1:3-14; Romans 8:18-39

For those of us whose lives are conditioned by the Western European cultural tradition, one of the complicating factors in understanding the cross is that it's everywhere. The cross has become so commonplace that it's little more than a part of the furniture, as familiar as the old sofa in the living room. If our Lenten journey is to lead us anywhere close to the revolutionary power of what the apostle Paul called "the message about the cross" (1 Corinthians 1:18), we need to be clear that we're not talking about the cross the way we generally see it. We're not singing with the poetic eloquence of John Bowring, who gloried in the cross "towering o'er the wrecks of time" while "all the light of sacred story gathers round its head sublime" ("In the Cross of Christ I Glory," written in 1825). We're not pointing to an architecturally appropriate cross on a high steeple or sanctuary wall. We're not describing the perfectly matched white crosses that stand at perfect attention in Arlington National Cemetery to mark the sacrifices of war. And we are not pricing crosses on the jewelry counter in the department store. The New Testament writers never could have imagined a designer-fashioned cross dangling around a debutante's neck or bouncing against a star athlete's perfectly chiseled chest.

The track we follow during Lent takes us to an ugly place of bloody, brutal execution; a stinking dung heap of naked humiliation, abject failure, and unmitigated defeat. Golgotha was unquestionably the worst place in the world for the track to run out. It was the last stop on the way to incomprehensibly miserable rejection and death. It was the form of capital punishment reserved for the worst political prisoners. It was specifically designed to maximize the humiliation of the criminal and to serve as a public warning to any would-be insurrectionists. New Testament scholar and theologian Jürgen Moltmann warned, "Christians who do not have the feeling that they must flee the crucified Christ have probably not yet understood him in a sufficiently radical way" (*The Crucified God,* New York: Harper & Row, 1974; page 38). We are talking about the very real suffering and death of Jesus on a very real cross—which, when you think about it, raises some very difficult questions for Christian believers.

The basic affirmation of the Christian faith is that Jesus of Nazareth was, in fact, the incarnate Son of God; the Word made flesh; the finite, human expression of the infinite, almighty God. The historical faith of the church declares that Jesus was as much of God as could be contained in human flesh. That affirmation was easy enough to believe in Advent, when we prepared for the coming of *Emmanuel,* which means "God with us." It seemed as clear as a star in the eastern sky when we lit our candles and sang "Silent Night" on Christmas Eve. It was joyfully apparent during Epiphany when we read the stories of Jesus healing the sick, teaching on the hillside, and calling disciples along the seashore.

But then along comes Ash Wednesday, with its dusty reminder that all our journeys end in death. We walk away from worship with the black smudge of a cross on our forehead and the disturbing words of the liturgy lingering in our ears: "Remember that you are dust, and to dust you shall return." We, like Jesus' first disciples, are surprised by his ominous warning that "the Son of Man must undergo great suffering, and be rejected by the elders, the chief priests, and the scribes, and be killed, and after three days rise again" (Mark 8:31). With them, we recoil from his challenge, "If any want to become my followers, let them deny themselves and take up their cross and follow me. For those who want to save their life will lose it, and those who lose their life for my sake, and for the sake of the gospel, will save it" (Mark 8:34-35). The realization begins to sink in that Jesus is determined to go to the cross, and he intends to take us with him!

All too suddenly, the joyful affirmation that Jesus is "God with us" stands in shocking contrast to the looming shadow of the cross, and an unsettling question begins to form in our soul. It's the kind of question that polite, "religious" folks often hesitate to ask. But folks whose experience with the cross has not been dulled by comfortable familiarity often blurt it out with an honesty that shatters any artificially pious veneer: *If Jesus is the Son of God, then what is he doing here, at the cross? What's a good person doing in a place like this? What is God doing when Jesus is rejected, beaten, bleeding, naked, and nailed to a cross? What is God doing at the cross?*

If we live with these questions long enough, they will probably lead us to an even more unsettling question: What is God doing *here*? What does the death of Jesus on the cross tell us about what God is doing in a world like this?

What is God doing in a world where very bad things still happen to very good people;

where love is still crucified by hate;

where generosity is still beaten down by greed;

where compassion is still done in by selfishness;

where love is still distorted by lust;

where justice is still perverted by prejudice;

where the promise of peace is still drowned out by the thunder of war;

where powerless love is still nailed to the cross by loveless power?

What is God doing in a world where terrorists fly jet airliners into the World Trade Center? Where is God when American jets drop thousands of bombs on Afghanistan? What is God doing about the ongoing conflict in the Middle East? What is God doing in a world where innocent children suffer and where good people face lonely, agonizing death? What is God doing here?

The Bible offers a bold answer to these questions. "In him," Paul declared, "we have redemption through his blood" (Ephesians 1:7). From cover to cover, the Bible declares that God is at work within human history to redeem the whole world. Very specifically, the New Testament declares that God was at work at the cross to redeem every last and lost one of us and to redeem and restore this bruised and broken creation. So, what on earth—literally "on earth"—does it mean to be redeemed?

When I think about the word *redemption,* my memory sails back to the days when "S & H Green Stamps" were a staple of our existence. It was also a time when a service-station bell would ring, and an attendant would come running out to pump your gas, clean your windshield, and check your oil! Businesses would give us stamps corresponding to the amount of our purchase. It was, I guess, an early version of frequent-flyer miles. We'd paste those stamps into little paperback books. When the books were filled, we would take them to what was called a Redemption Center. There, we could trade in our books of stamps for all sorts of things. I was always attracted to the big items, but we never seemed to have enough stamps to get more than a toaster! The Redemption Center was the place where we traded something that had almost no value—the stamps—for something of significantly greater value.

A trip to the "Redemption Center" at least moves us in the direction of the biblical meaning of *redemption.* One of its roots was in the slave culture of ancient times and the practice of manumission, by which a person could buy slaves in order to give them their freedom. *Redemption* was the process by which a price was paid for a slave to be set free. The redemption price was often paid at the pagan temple to symbolize that the freed slave no longer belonged to a slaveholder, but now belonged to the god of that temple. Because slaves were generally unable to pay the price of their freedom themselves, they were usually redeemed by the action of another person.

The biblical writers picked up this image to describe the way

24

God redeems his people. The decisive moment in the Old Testament was when God redeemed a large group of helpless Hebrew slaves from bondage in Egypt. God led them to a land where they could live in freedom and fulfill the purpose for which they had been created.

The early Christians drew from the long tradition of biblical faith when they looked back at what God had done at the cross and said that they felt as if they had been redeemed. The love of God revealed at the cross and the power of God demonstrated in the resurrection of Jesus had released them from bondage to sin and death. They felt as if they had been set free from the narrow confines of selfishness, greed, guilt, violence, and despair and had been given a whole new life. They said that the price of their redemption had been paid in the death of God's own Son. So, Paul declared, "In him we have redemption through his blood, the forgiveness of our trespasses, according to the riches of his grace that he lavished on us" (Ephesians 1:7-8). The New Testament declares that at the cross, God was giving his only Son, Jesus, to redeem each of us.

Paul's letter to the Ephesians lifts God's redemptive action at a specific moment in time, on a Friday afternoon somewhere around A.D. 33, into the larger framework of God's timeless purpose of saving love. Paul declares that God "chose us in Christ before the foundation of the world to be holy and blameless before him in love" (Ephesians 1:4). Paul sees the love of God in Christ as "a plan for the fullness of time" (1:10). This means that the cross was not a patch-and-repair job on a broken creation. It was the definitive moment in time that defines for all time the timeless character of God. David Buttrick, who teaches preachers at Vanderbilt School of Theology, writes:

> God's attributes—omnipotence, omniscience, omnipresence, perfection—are all redefined by the broken body of the crucified Christ. God's self-abnegating love, a willing-to-die love, is written across all time and space. So the cross is not a desperate concession, something almighty God is forced to do because nothing else seems to work; no, the cross is consistent with God's faithfulness from the beginning. Here is a God who all along has been

willing to be impotent, to not know, to suffer with, to die for a people, a dearly loved people. . . . God's glory is nothing less than the glory of self-giving love.

(*The Mystery of the Passion*, Minneapolis: Fortress Press, 1992; page 129)

The cross is the decisive demonstration of the essential nature and character of God. Let me share with you a very human example of the meaning of redemption. A family's son went off to college a couple of years ago. During his first year away from home, the young man became severely depressed. He started drinking and ended up using drugs. Finally, he dropped out of school and came home. When they got him into therapy to figure out what was going on, they discovered that as a child he had been sexually molested by a teenage babysitter. The secret had been buried so deeply within his psyche that even he did not realize how it controlled and enslaved him.

Now, what would his parents do? The two persons who had loved him since before he was born invested everything they had in trying to save him. They used up their savings. They took out a second mortgage on a piece of property. They have spent long hours with him in therapy. Because they love him, they are paying a very high price to set him free and to enable him to live the life for which he was born. When, by God's grace, this young man has been set free from this bondage, we will all say that he has been redeemed.

That's what God was doing at the cross. The infinite love of the infinite God was giving of itself in finite space and time to redeem this finite and infinitely loved creation.

The New Testament proclaims God's redemption as a present reality. The apostle Paul said, "We *have* redemption through his blood" (Ephesians 1:7, emphasis added). God's action in the past becomes a present experience for every person who receives by faith the gift of God's self-giving love and unde-served grace. The good news of the gospel is that we can know that we have been redeemed. People in the Methodist tradition celebrate the turning point in John Wesley's spiritual journey. It came on May 24, 1738, when he said that he felt his heart "strangely warmed" by an inner assurance that Christ had forgiven his sins. His personal and present assurance of God's redeeming love ignited the spiritual awakening of the Wesleyan revival in the eighteenth century and gave birth to the Methodist movement around the world. Methodism was born in an Anglican priest's present awareness of his redemption in Jesus Christ.

We see God's redeeming love in the past at the cross of Christ. We experience that redeeming love in the present by faith. But Paul says that we also await the completion of God's redemption in the future. In the same way that God was at work at the cross, God is at work in the present to redeem the whole creation in the future. Paul announces the promise of "our inheritance toward redemption as God's own people" (Ephesians 1:14). He uses a word that describes the way an accountant totals up the accounts, when he describes the way God intends "to gather up all things in him, things in heaven and things on earth" (1:10). And God's redemption isn't just for individual human beings. God is at work to gather up the whole sin-broken creation in Jesus Christ. In his letter to the Romans, Paul declared:

> For the creation waits with eager longing for the revealing of the children of God . . . in hope that the creation itself will be set free from its bondage to decay and will obtain the freedom of the glory of the children of God.   (Romans 8:19-21)

As I was working on writing this study, I told a fellow pastor that I was having a hard time trying to squeeze one of the biggest concepts in Scripture into messages that I felt would connect with readers. He listened and then replied, "Ah, I'm sure it will all come together." And I said, "That's exactly what Paul says God is up to!"

God looks at this broken, abused, pain-filled, suffering world and says, "I'm sure it will come together." Through the self-giving love that was revealed at the cross, God is at work to gather up all things in Christ, to bring all things together the way God

27

intended from the first dawn of creation. Jesus taught us to pray for God's kingdom to come and for God's will to be done on earth, even as it is already fulfilled in heaven. We live with confidence that through the sacrificial love of God in Christ, "the kingdom of the world has become the kingdom of our Lord / and of his Messiah, / and he will reign forever and ever" (Revelation 11:15). We look with hope to "the holy city, the new Jerusalem, coming down out of heaven from God, prepared as a bride adorned for her husband. . . . 'He will dwell with them [as their God]; / they will be his peoples, / and God himself will be with them; / he will wipe every tear from their eyes. / Death will be no more; / mourning and crying and pain will be no more, / for the first things have passed away' " (21:2-4). We dare to work toward the day when "they shall beat their swords into plowshares, / and their spears into pruning hooks; / nation shall not lift up sword against nation, / neither shall they learn war any more" (Isaiah 2:4).

New Testament scholar Richard B. Hayes pinpoints the church's role in this "in between" time—this time between God's redemption at the cross and the fulfillment of God's ultimate redemption of creation—when he writes that "the Spirit-endowed church stands within the present age as a sign of what is to come, already prefiguring the redemption for which it awaits. . . . [T]he church embodies in its life together the world-reconciling love of Jesus Christ . . . the church . . . is a sneak preview of God's ultimate redemption of the world" (*The Moral Vision of the New Testament,* San Francisco: HarperSan-Francisco, 1996; pages 21, 24). We are called to be the present witness of the same redemptive love that was revealed at the cross and that will be fulfilled in the end of time. We are called to be the agents of the redemptive love that sent Jesus to the cross.

What's a good God doing at the cross? What is a good God doing in a world like this? God *was* and *is* at work to redeem every last and lost one of us. The cross is the place where we can be redeemed. This world is the arena in which we become a part of God's ongoing work of redemption.

Questions for Discussion and Reflection

1. How do you experience the cross? What do you think or feel when you see a cross?

2. What images come into your mind when you hear or reflect on the word *redemption*?

3. How have you experienced what the biblical writers described when they used the word *redeemed*?

4. What evidence do you see for the affirmation that God is at work to save and redeem this whole creation?

Prayer

O God, in awe we see your great act of redemption at the cross. In faith we receive your redeeming grace into our lives. In hope we anticipate its fulfillment in us and in the whole creation. Amen.

Why Did Jesus Die on the Cross? To Cleanse from Sin: Do You Want to Be Clean?

Luke 5:12-13; Ephesians 5:25-26; 1 John 1:5–2:2

In his book *Love Beyond Reason,* John Ortberg reminded me of the most dreaded of all childhood diseases. More dangerous than polio, more contagious than measles, the mere mention of the name was enough to send brave little boys running to the other side of the playground in fear. Things seemed to change around the time we got to sixth or seventh grade, but until that adolescent explosion in our glands, girls were simply crawling with this condition. It was so contagious that we would shout the name so that others would not be contaminated by it: *"Cooties! She has cooties!"* (See *Love Beyond Reason,* New York: HarperCollins, 1998; page 48.)

Though it might have seemed a momentary tragedy to be accused of having cooties, no one, as far as we can tell, ever came to any real harm from this imaginary ailment. Unfortunately, the same cannot be said about a true-to-life counterpart that, especially in biblical times, caused its sufferers to pay a heavy price. Most scholars agree that when the Bible speaks of *leprosy,* it is referring to a broad assortment of diseases, not just the one we know today as Hansen's disease. These diseases had several things in common. Most were recognized by a skin ailment. All were thought to be contagious, although it turns out that many were not. And all of them marked the afflicted person as being ritually unclean. The result was that lepers, as they were called, were isolated from the community, cut off from their family and friends, excluded from the Temple, and forced to survive in total rejection by everyone around them. When they came near other people, they were required to shout, "Unclean!" (Leviticus 13:45-46).

The biblical stigma associated with leprosy continues to this day. Chris was a muscular, good-looking, twenty-five-year-old guy from California. He usually told people that he had injured his hand lifting weights, and they usually believed him. The truth is that he had leprosy. "I just blurted it out one day," he reported. "I said I had leprosy. I didn't think they would react that way, moving away from me. For a while, I tried to take back what I had said to them. I said I was just joking. But now I know you just don't tell anyone" (*The Orlando Sentinel*, December 27, 1991; page A-7).

In the Old Testament, leprosy was just one of a long list of things that could cause a person, place, or thing to be considered unclean. Being unclean, it was believed, separated people from the holiness, goodness, and purity of God. It was an outward and visible sign of an inward and spiritual alienation from God. Therefore, an unclean person had to be ritually cleansed before he or she could come in contact with other people or could come into the synagogue.

The whole, long biblical tradition regarding uncleanness is in the background of one of the most shocking things Jesus ever did. If the story doesn't shock us, it's because we are almost incapable of feeling all that it meant to be considered unclean. According to Luke, the physician, the man in this story was "covered with leprosy." He didn't just have a minor case; he was crawling with it. Luke says that "when he saw Jesus, he bowed with his face to the ground and begged him, 'Lord, if you choose, you can make me clean'" (Luke 5:12). It would have blown the mind of everyone who saw it when "Jesus stretched out his hand, touched him, and said, 'I do choose. Be made clean.'" Dr. Luke records, "Immediately the leprosy left him" (verse 13).

The shocker was not just *that* Jesus healed this leper, but *how*

Jesus healed him. There was no question in the man's mind that Jesus *could* heal him. The question was whether Jesus *would* heal a person who was unclean. The surprise is not just that Jesus healed the leper, but that he did it by touching him. According to the ritual law, Jesus made himself unclean when he touched this man to make him clean.

I'm sure you have heard of Murphy's Law. It says that if anything can go wrong, it will. I have it on the full authority of one of my Internet-surfing friends that there is another law known as Imbesi's Law of the Conservation of Filth. Imbesi's Law says that in order for something to become clean, something else must become dirty. And it is, of course, observably true.

I have an old, corduroy-covered, over-stuffed chair and ottoman in my study. By old, I mean that I've rescued it from the parsonage garage sale more than once. It's a lot like Marty Crane's chair on the television show *Frasier*. One of the reasons I like my chair is that the arm is just wide enough to hold my coffee cup. But as you would guess, every now and then I jump up to answer the phone and knock the cup off the arm, thereby spilling it onto the light beige carpet. This always seems to fulfill another law that says that you will only spill a coffee cup when it's more than half full, the corollary of which is that if toast with butter and jelly is dropped on the floor, it always falls with the jelly side down. My wife is one of those people who believe that the Bible would be a better book if it actually said that cleanliness is next to Godliness. When the coffee catastrophe happens, she does not like it one little bit! She keeps asking the utterly irrelevant question, "Why do you put your coffee cup on the arm of the chair where it can so easily be knocked off?"

The coffee catastrophe happens just often enough that I have become rather adept at moving very quickly (and very quietly!) to grab an old bath towel from the rag box in the laundry room to soak up the coffee before it leaves a permanent stain on the carpet. The only problem is that I'm left with an old bath towel that now bears the brown stains of soaked-up coffee. My wife inevitably finds it in the laundry basket, and I'm nabbed again, thereby proving the Bible correct when it says that our sins will find us out! Imbesi's Law is observably true. In order for something to become clean, something else must become dirty. The stain has to go somewhere.

The Bible says that spiritual uncleanness in your life and in mine is the result of sin. Sin is anything that causes alienation between us and God, or between us and others. It is anything that separates us, cuts us off, and isolates us from holy living and loving relationships that model the holiness and the love of God. Sin always leaves us feeling unclean. William Shakespeare knew his Bible. In his dramatic commentary on the effect of human guilt for sin, Macbeth, unable to remove the stain of blood from his own hands, watches the insane Lady Macbeth wander through the darkened castle, desperately attempting to wipe her hands clean. Macbeth pleads with the physician to help his wife "cleanse the stuff'd bosom of that perilous stuff / Which weighs upon the heart" (*Macbeth*, Act 5, Scene 3). But the Macbeths cannot remove the stain from their own hands. The stain has to go somewhere. For one thing to be clean, something else must get dirty.

In the sacrificial system of the Old Testament, the stain of human sin was transferred from the people to the lamb that was sacrificed on the altar. In that ritual action, the people were cleansed of their sin by the blood of the lamb. Once a year, on Yom Kippur, the "Day of Atonement," the high priest would place his hands on the head of the goat while confessing the sins of the people, thereby transferring their sin onto the goat. The goat was then driven out into the desert so that it became known as the scapegoat, the one who carried their sin away.

The Hebrews knew that we all do "picture thinking." We need strong visual images to convey profound spiritual truth. We need outward and visible signs of an inward and spiritual reality. The sacrificial rituals provided powerful visual images of the meaning of atonement. They conveyed to the people the way God would deal with their sin and would take away their uncleanness. Those dramatic visual images linger in the background of that moment when Jesus stretched out his hand and touched this man with leprosy. Jesus' choice to take the man's uncleanness onto himself so that the man would be made clean was a dramatic image of the way God's saving action was to be accomplished.

When the early Christians tried to describe the difference the death of Jesus had made in their lives, they said they felt as if they had been made clean. As they attempted to explain to an unbelieving world what God had done at the cross, they said that the guilt and the stain of their sin had been taken up into the self-giving love of God, and, like the leper, they had been made clean. Paul declared the good news of Christ's cleansing power to the Ephesians when he wrote, "Christ loved the church and gave himself up for her, in order to make her holy by cleansing her with the washing of water by the word, so as to present the church to himself in splendor, without a spot or wrinkle or anything of the kind—yes, so that she may be holy and without blemish" (Ephesians 5:25-27).

Why did Jesus die on the cross? One of the biblical answers is that he died to cleanse us of our sin. Paul says that Jesus loved us so much that he gave himself for us to make us holy. Like the lamb on the altar or the scapegoat in the desert, he took our uncleanness on himself so that we could be made clean. Like the blood of the lamb, the sacrificial love of God revealed in the blood of Jesus on the cross has the power to make us clean. The visual power of the biblical imagery comes down to us in two classic gospel hymns. William Cowper used it when he wrote

There is a fountain filled with blood drawn from Emmanuel's
     veins;
  And sinners plunged beneath that flood lose all their guilty
     stains.
               ("There Is a Fountain Filled with Blood," 1771)

Robert Lowry expressed it in a question and answer:

What can wash away my sin? Nothing but the blood of Jesus.
  What can make me whole again? Nothing but the blood of
     Jesus.
O precious is the flow that makes me bright as snow;
  No other fount I know; nothing but the blood of Jesus.
               ("Nothing but the Blood," 1876)

34

Blood imagery was a familiar theme for Christian people in the eighteenth and nineteenth centuries, but things have changed. Kathleen Norris captured the feeling of many contemporary Christians when she said that in most mainline congregations, the only folks who appreciate hymns with language about the blood are kids like her nine-year-old nephew, who find in them "a welcome opportunity to be 'totally grossed out' in church." Across most of the twentieth century, most mainline churches tended to shy away from the blood language of the Bible. But Norris said that this hesitation is our loss. "Christians have grown adept at finding ways to disincarnate the religion, resisting the scandalous notion that what is holy can have much to do with the muck and smell of a stable, the painful agony of death on a cross. The Incarnation remains a scandal to anyone who wants religion to be a purely spiritual matter, an etherized, bloodless bliss" (*Amazing Grace*, New York: Riverhead Books, 1998; page 114). Reality, however, has a way of catching up with us. Back in the sanitized mentality of the mid-twentieth century, we may have been able to avoid talking about "power in the blood." But then along came Ryan White, Arthur Ashe, and AIDS. When was the last time a nurse took your blood or a dentist cleaned your teeth without wearing latex gloves? We know that there is, in fact, power in the blood. We know that it can be the power of life and death.

The biblical images of blood are rooted in the belief that blood carried life. In the sacrificial traditions of the Old Testament, an unclean person was made clean by the shedding of the blood of the lamb. Lepers were unclean (and actually were considered dead) until they were sprinkled with the blood. It symbolized that they had been given life by the death of another in the giving of the blood. The Bible says that at the cross, Jesus took all our uncleanness, everything that alienates us from God and from one another, into himself. Like the lamb on the altar, he died so that we could be made clean. In the symbol of his blood, we experience the power of divine love that gives us new life.

According to my Internet-surfing friend, there is a corollary to Imbesi's Law called Freeman's Extension. It says that you can get everything dirty without getting anything clean. Again, this is a law that is observably true.

Have you noticed how easy it is to spread dirt around but never get clean? Have you noticed how often we would rather spread our "dirt" around on other people than take responsibility for it ourselves? Have you noticed how quickly we can point out the stain in someone else's life, and how slow we are to acknowledge the stain in our own? Have you noticed how easy it is to get everything else dirty but never to get really clean?

The truth about your life and mine is that the only way to get clean is to acknowledge that we are dirty. The Bible calls the process by which we acknowledge the dirt in our lives "confession." It's what we hear in the First Epistle of John. Watch for the contrasting use of the word *if* in this passage.

> This is the message we have heard from him and proclaim to you, that God is light and in him there is no darkness at all. If we say that we have fellowship with him while we are walking in darkness, we lie and do not do what is true; but if we walk in the light as he himself is in the light, we have fellowship with one another, and the blood of Jesus his Son cleanses us from all sin. If we say that we have no sin, we deceive ourselves, and the truth is not in us. If we confess our sins, he who is faithful and just will forgive us our sins and cleanse us from all unrighteousness. If we say that we have not sinned, we make him a liar, and his word is not in us.
>
> My little children, I am writing these things to you so that you may not sin. But if anyone does sin, we have an advocate with the Father, Jesus Christ the righteous; and he is the atoning sacrifice for our sins, and not for ours only but also for the sins of the whole world. (1 John 1:5-2:2)

The only way to get clean is to confess that we are dirty and to come to the One who chooses to cleanse us by taking our uncleanness into himself. Do you have any idea how much courage it took for that man who was covered with leprosy to make his way into the village that day, to watch for Jesus, and then to fall down in front of him and say, "If you choose, you can make me clean"? Do you have any idea how much courage it takes for folks like us, folks who look so neat and clean on the outside, to acknowledge the stains on the inside of our lives? Do you know how much courage it takes to face the things that alienate us from God and separate us from one another? Do you know how much sheer courage it takes to confess our sin?

But here's the promise: If we confess our sin, God is faithful and God is just and God will forgive our sin and cleanse us from all unrighteousness. The good news for your life and mine is that God is still in the soul-cleaning business today! All we need to do is confess our need and receive the gift.

In his fantasy story *The Great Divorce,* C. S. Lewis takes a busload of residents from hell on a day trip to heaven. One of the visitors is surprised to find a resident of heaven who he knew had committed murder on earth. The visitor protests, "I'd have thought you and I ought to be the other way round." He goes on to defend his own life:

> "Look at me, now," said the Ghost, slapping its chest (but the slap made no noise). "I gone straight all my life. I don't say I was a religious man and I don't say I had no faults, far from it. But I done my best all my life, see? I done my best by everyone, that's the sort of chap I was. I never asked for anything that wasn't mine by rights. . . . I got to have my rights same as you, see?"

The murderer, who is now a resident of heaven, replies, "Oh no. It's not as bad as that. I haven't got my rights, or I should not be here. You will not get yours either. You'll get something far better." But the Ghost visitor continues his protest, "I only want my rights. I'm not asking for anybody's bleeding charity." To which the Heavenly Ghost replies, "Then do. At once. Ask for the Bleeding Charity. Everything is here for the asking and nothing can be bought" (New York: Touchstone, 1996; pages 34-5).

For all I know, Lewis's description of heavenly mercy might have been influenced by the way William Shakespeare described mercy as "an attribute to God himself." In *The Merchant of Venice,* Portia says, "Though justice be thy plea, / consider this, / That, in the course of justice none of us / Should see salvation: we do pray for mercy" (Act 4, Scene 1). The cleansing we most deeply need is found in the mercy that we never can earn. It is offered to us as a gift of God's infinite grace, received through confession, prayer, and faith.

Although years have passed and she now lives in another part of the country, her face came to mind as I worked on this chapter. She wasn't a member of our church. She had never, in fact, been inside the building when she called and asked if she could see me. She came into the office with the same urgency of that man with leprosy who bowed before Jesus.

She had no interest in small talk. I had barely gotten her name when she began to pour out her story. She dumped it out on the office floor the way a person dumps dirty laundry into the washer. She had grown up in the faith, but she felt alienated from God. She hid it most of the time, but she was having a hard time connecting with other people. Hidden in her past were a string of shattered relationships and broken promises. There was a teenage abortion. There were misguided decisions and, at some places, outright rejection of some of her deepest values. She confessed it all before me, but more important, she confessed it before God. Above the sofa in my office is a print of Salvador Dali's painting of *The Christ of St. John of the Cross.* I remember her sitting beneath it as if she were pouring out her life story at the foot of the cross.

I listened. I prayed. Then she prayed and confessed it all to God. When she finished her prayer, I quoted John's words: "If we confess our sins, he is faithful and just and will forgive our sins and cleanse us from all unrighteousness" (1 John 1:9). Then she lifted her head, opened her eyes, and with tears of joy running down her cheeks, smiled, and said, "I feel clean!"

There is good news for the "cootie-infested" kid within each of us. There is good news for everyone who is sick and tired of feeling unclean. Christ loved you so much that he gave himself up for you, in order to make you holy by cleansing you with the washing of water by the Word, so that he could present you to himself in splendor, without a spot or wrinkle or anything of the kind. The Bible has good news for every one of us who needs to be made clean. Here's the promise, direct from the God who loves you: If we confess our sin, he is faithful and just and will forgive our sin and cleanse us from all unrighteousness. Christ died to make you clean!

Questions for Discussion and Reflection

1. How do the biblical images of uncleanness speak to you?

2. When have you felt that you were unclean? What did it take—or what *would* it take—for you to receive new life or to be made clean again?

3. How do you respond to the biblical image of the blood of Christ? What are your thoughts on the words of the hymns that are quoted in this chapter?

4. How have you experienced the cleansing mercy of God?

Prayer

Holy God, it's hard for us to acknowledge that we are dirty and that the cleansing we need is the mercy we can never earn. Cleanse us by the blood of your Son, and may we be truly clean. Amen.

Why Did Jesus Die on the Cross? To Take Our Place: Did He Really Die for Me?

1 Peter 2:24-25; Isaiah 52:13–53:12

Surfing the Internet not long ago, I came across the lyrics to a song that I remembered from the pre-Vatican II world of my adolescence. Those were the days when you could pick out the faithful Roman Catholics on the highway by the presence of a small, white, plastic statue of Jesus attached to the dashboard of their car. It was supposed to protect them from danger, though I never saw a statistical study to prove it. My guess is that careless drivers who had Jesus on their dashboard were just about as likely to have an accident as careless drivers who didn't. According to this Web site, a group called The Gold Coast Singers recorded the song. I didn't remember the group, but I remembered the words.

> I don't care if it rains or freezes,
> 's long as I've got my Plastic Jesus.

The Roman Catholics have pretty much done away with Plastic Jesus. That's a good thing. There is nothing plastic or artificial about the Jesus we meet on the way to the cross.

He's really human and really one of us. The gospel offers no guarantee that we will be protected from the risk, danger, or pain of a sometimes-hostile world. In fact, the only promise Jesus makes is that those who come after him will share his

40

rejection, suffering, and death so that they might also share the new life of his resurrection. The track we are following takes us into the deepest realities of human suffering and pain.

People who know a lot more about William Shakespeare than I do say that *King Lear* is his greatest play. The sheer passion and immense human tragedy of the interconnected stories make it nearly as exhausting for the audience to watch as it is for the actors to perform. During the emotionally constrained Victorian era in England, some theater critics said that *King Lear* should never be performed in public because it was too painful to watch. Since it was first written, the play has both attracted and repelled its audiences.

Isn't there something of that same attraction and aversion with most tragedy? We are drawn into it and repelled by it at the same time. There is something about it that draws us in even as we pull away. My daughter who is in the television news business tells me that the rule of thumb in the newsroom is, "If it bleeds, it leads." We may criticize the media for showing human suffering and pain, but we can't take our eyes off it, either.

In the same way, when we strip away all the artificial trappings and look at the cross in all its naked, gruesome reality, we are both drawn to it and repelled by it. I read recently about a decision by a state education department in Australia that banned a passion play, not because of its religious content, but because an education official said the state could not tolerate that level of violence in the schools (*The Christian Century*, March 7, 2001; page 13). I could not help but wonder how that school board handled all of the violence in Shakespeare. In *King Lear*, for instance, the Earl of Gloucester's eyes are plucked out. (I warned you that this is not an easy play!) When Lear asks him how he sees the world without his eyes, Gloucester replies, "I see it feelingly."

To "see it feelingly" is the best way I know to see the passion and death of our Lord. Almost every year during Lent I come across an article in a journal or magazine in which a physician analyzes the gruesome medical details of death by crucifixion. The writer describes the placement of the nails, the amount of blood that was lost, and the way the condemned prisoner died slowly by asphyxiation. To tell you the truth, I am both drawn to those articles and repelled by them. We can study it. We can analyze it. We can make our stumbling attempts to explain it. But the closer we get to Good Friday, the more I know that the only way to experience its life-changing power is to see it feelingly; to allow the power of God's self-giving love at the cross to soak into some deep place in our souls that is beyond the ability of our brains to explain or our minds to contain. The New Testament writers are not as interested in our objective analysis of the cross as they are in our subjective experience of it. To feel our way into the story is to sense that we are a part of what happened there.

The track we are following is leading us through the ways in which faithful people have attempted to describe "theories of the atonement." They are human attempts to comprehend the way the death of Jesus on the cross brings "at-one-ment" between rebellious, sin-addicted human beings and a righteous God whose whole being is oriented toward reconciliation. We turn in this chapter to what theologians call "substitutionary atonement." This interpretation of Jesus' death on the cross is both widely accepted and deeply resisted. Professor S. Mark Heim summarized it this way:

> We are guilty of sin against God and our neighbors. The continuing sins themselves, the root desires that prompt them, and the guilt we bear for making such brutal response to God's good gifts—all these together separate us from God and are far beyond any human power to mend. . . . [A] gap, a price, remains to be reckoned with. Christ stands in this gap, pays this price, bearing the punishment we deserve and he does not. . . . Christ offers something on our behalf that could never be expected or required, Christ offers the "over and above" gift that clears the slate and brings sinners into reconciled relation with God.
> ("Christ Crucified," *The Christian Century*, March 7, 2001; page 13)

The New Testament claims that Jesus took our place on the cross. This affirmation is proclaimed with stunning clarity in

1 Peter 2:24: "He himself bore our sins in his body on the cross, so that, free from sins, we might live for righteousness; by his wounds you have been healed." Christian people declare that Jesus died for us, for all of us, for each of us. On the cross, the One who was all of God that could be squeezed into human form took into himself all the things that alienate us from God and from one another in order to make us one with God, one with others, and one with ourselves.

Peter was drawing on a powerful word picture from the Old Testament prophecy of Isaiah. It's known as the "Song of the Suffering Servant" and is found in Isaiah 52:13–53:12. I encourage you to take a moment to read these words in your Bible, with feeling, allowing your imagination to paint the picture inside your soul.

One of the most powerful commentaries on Isaiah's vision of the suffering servant was not written by a scholar, but painted by an artist. His name was Mathias Grünewald. In 1513, he was commissioned by the monks of Saint Anthony to paint a new altarpiece for the chapel in their hospital at Isenheim, Germany. The monks specialized in treating the poorest victims of the many plagues that swept across Europe in the sixteenth century. The patients who came to their door knew that it was the last step along a journey toward a painful death.

The ruthless agony of Grünewald's portrayal of the crucified Jesus shocked and appalled some folks, particularly those who were not patients. Some art historians have called it the most grotesque portrayal of the cross to emerge from the Renaissance. The sky is dark and ominous. Jesus' body is stretched taut. Huge nails in his hands send his fingers into a sort of electric shock. But the most disturbing detail of the painting is the way Grünewald covered the body of Jesus with lacerations and bleeding sores. They were, in fact, the same type of sores that marked the bodies of many of the dying patients who gathered in the chapel for worship.

Grünewald wanted the patients to see a Jesus who was acquainted with their infirmity. He wanted them to experience the presence of a dying Savior from whom some people would hide their faces. He enabled them to know the love of a God who had borne their infirmities and carried their diseases. He dared to focus our eyes on a Jesus who was wounded for our transgressions and crushed for our iniquities. His painting draws us into the presence of the One whose punishment can make us whole and by whose bruises we are healed. Grünewald portrayed what German theologian Jürgen Moltmann described when he said that "suffering is overcome by suffering, and wounds are healed by wounds." He taught that healing comes through "the suffering of love, which is not afraid of what is sick and ugly, but accepts it and takes it to itself in order to heal it" (*The Crucified God;* New York: Harper & Row, 1974; page 46).

After spending more than three hours in the presence of Grünewald's "The Crucifixion," Henri Nouwen wrote to his nephew, "When I saw Grünewald's paintings of the tortured, naked body of Jesus, I realized anew that the cross isn't just a beautiful piece of art . . . ; it is the sign of the most radical transformation in our manner of thinking, feeling, and living. Jesus' death on the cross has changed everything" (*Letter to Marc About Jesus,* Harper and Row, 1987; page 28).

Legend has it that Vladimir Horowitz, the great concert pianist, once played a Beethoven sonata in a university classroom. When he finished, a student threw up his hand and asked, "What does it mean?" Without a word, Horowitz sat back down at the piano and played it again. In the same way, if a Jewish rabbi in Jesus' time had been asked, "What does Isaiah mean?" he probably would have turned back to the "Suffering Servant" text and read it all again. But since I am not a rabbi, in another good rabbinical tradition, I'll tell you another story. The story is just as impossible to verify as it is to disbelieve.

Several decades after the Civil War, there was an old man who came almost every day to visit the grave of a Confederate solider in a small Southern town. The odd thing was that no one in town could make any connection between the name on the gravestone and the name of the man who visited it. But he kept coming, day after day, to pause in a moment of silence and then go on his way. Finally, someone asked why he kept coming to that grave. The man said that when the war broke out, he was the only son in his family. There was a process by which a family who needed their son at home could send someone else into the army and provide the cost for his provisions. The old man pointed down at the soldier's grave and said, "This is the man who took my place. He died at Gettysburg so that I could live."

How Jesus could take our place on the cross is beyond me. I cannot rationally explain it to you. I cannot fully make sense of it myself. When it comes to substitutionary theology, I am both repelled by it and drawn into it. But I know that when I see it feelingly, when I allow it to penetrate into some deep place in my soul, I know that "all we like sheep have gone astray." All of us have turned to our own way. And somehow I know that Jesus bore our sins in his body on the cross so that, set free from sin, we might live the life God intended for us to live. I know that the only hope for healing for our bruised and broken souls, and for this bruised and broken world, is the self-giving love revealed at the cross. I know that when we turn back to this Shepherd of our souls, the love of God at the cross can heal the brokenness in our lives.

It blows my mind. But I'm in good company, because it blew Charles Wesley's mind, too. He never got over it. All of his hymns on the passion and death of Jesus have a sense of awestricken amazement in them. In one of them, he gasps a breathless question to God:

> O Love divine, what hast thou done!
> The immortal God hath died for me!
> The Father's co-eternal Son
> bore all my sins upon the tree.
> Th' immortal God for me hath died:
> My Lord, my Love, is crucified!
>
> . . . .
> Behold him, all ye that pass by,
> the bleeding Prince of life and peace!
> Come, sinners, see your Savior die,
> and say, "Was ever grief like his?"
> Come, feel with me his blood applied:
> My Lord, my Love, is crucified!
> ("O Love Divine, What Hast Thou Done," 1742)

45

One of the most memorable lessons Dr. Robert Traina taught was not in the seminary classroom, but in the chapel. Dr. Traina was our English Bible professor and the academic dean of our seminary. He was a clear-headed scholar who expected us to work our brains and who challenged us to think our way through the biblical texts with near-scientific accuracy. We generally experienced him to be a rather unemotional sort of academic, who was not easily moved by the sob stories that some students would offer when they had not completed their assignments. Much of his own training and scholarship had been focused on the atonement, and he could discuss all of the traditional theories with crystal clarity.

It was Good Friday. The seminary community had gathered in the chapel for the traditional three-hour service of worship, remembering the three hours that Jesus hung on the cross. As I remember it, Dr. Traina was the last preacher to speak on "The Seven Last Words" of Christ. (He is, in fact, the *only* preacher from that day that I remember.)

I don't actually remember the content of his sermon, but I remember that he came to the end and started to quote Charles Wesley's hymn. He completed the first line, "O Love divine, what hast thou done!" Then, as he began to quote the second line, we were all amazed when he paused to choke back his tears as he said, "The immortal God hath died for me!" Suddenly, we were moved beyond academic reflection about the cross, to a personal experience of it. Dr. Traina had experienced what it meant for a person to "see it feelingly." And in turn, so did we.

Questions for Discussion and Reflection

1. Read 1 Peter 2:24 again, this time inserting first-person singular pronouns: "He himself bore *my* sins in his body on the cross, so that, free from sins, *I* might live for righteousness; by his wounds *I* have been healed." How does that change in pronouns affect your reading of this verse? Read Isaiah 53:1-6 again, inserting first-person singular pronouns in the same way.

2. What difference would it make for you to "see it feelingly"

as you reflect on the cross? What is there about the cross that touches you at some place deeper than perhaps you can explain?

3. What particular image—for example, a painting; stained glass; words from Scripture or some other text—intensely speaks to you of Jesus' suffering and sacrifice on the cross? Explain why. If possible, find a copy of Matthias Grünewald's Isenheim altarpiece called "The Crucifixion" (you might try searching for it on the Internet), and reflect upon it, sharing your thoughts and feelings with someone else if you are comfortable doing so.

4. What difference does it make in your life and faith to say that Jesus took your place? When have you seen the cross "feelingly"?

Prayer

O Love Divine, we stumble before the mystery of the cross. May we feel in our souls the truth that our minds can never fully explain, and thereby know the Christ who died for us. Amen.

Why Did Jesus Die on the Cross? To Reconcile: How God Puts Humpty Dumpty Together Again

2 Corinthians 5:14-21; Colossians 1:15-23

Jesus said that we need to be like little children to enter the kingdom of God. More recently, Robert Fulghum reminded us that *All I Really Need to Know I Learned in Kindergarten*. So perhaps the place to begin in this chapter is with a children's nursery rhyme and an egg named Humpty Dumpty. You already know his sad story.

> Humpty Dumpty sat on a wall,
> Humpty Dumpty had a great fall.
> All the king's horses,
> And all the king's men,
> Couldn't put Humpty together again.

The nursery rhyme leaves some pretty significant questions unanswered. How did that egg get up on the wall in the first place? He certainly didn't climb up there by himself! Who is really behind this tragic event? Who is ultimately responsible for his fall? Who pushed him off that wall? Or was it a *her*? Humpty is not exactly a gender-specific name. Lawyers would be prone to ask if the builders of the wall had liability insurance. Why weren't there protective railings in place? Were warning notices about the danger of the fall posted at appropriate locations along the wall? And who is responsible for cleaning up the mess that was left? None of those questions is answered. All we get is a yucky pile of broken eggshell, floating around in a runny mess of egg white that will start stinking if someone doesn't clean it up.

It's really a rather dismal little ditty, this rhyme. Mother Goose leaves us with scrambled egg all over the place, and no hope of Humpty being put back together again. I kept thinking that there must be another verse somewhere that no one knows, like the second verse of "The Star-Spangled Banner." It's a children's nursery rhyme, after all; it ought to have a happy ending! But that's all there is; once on the wall, having had a great fall, all the money and power that was humanly available couldn't put Humpty Dumpty together again.

It would be nothing more than a gloomy little nursery rhyme except for one thing. The Bible says that it's *our* story, and that it happens to be true. The Creation narratives in Genesis (Chapters 1 and 2) say that we human beings were created, male and female, in the image of God. And the psalmist says that God made human beings just a little lower than the angels (Psalm 8:5, King James Version). (*There's* a height that would have left Humpty Dumpty's head spinning!)

But the Bible also says that we took a great fall. It says that all of us have sinned and have fallen short of the glory of God (Romans 3:23). All of us have fallen off the wall of God's good, loving, life-giving intention for our creation. You can read the evidence of it in the headlines on any day, at any time, in any place. There are broken lives, broken promises, broken relationships, broken nations, broken hopes, broken dreams, and broken hearts all over the place. And with all of our wisdom, and all of our strength, and all of our power, and all of our might, we've never been able to put them back together again.

The Bible does answer one of the questions Mother Goose left unanswered. The Bible tells us who did it: *We* did! And we *do*! The Bible says that the root cause of all the broken stuff in our lives and in our world is a ruthless, self-centered arrogance that refuses to allow God to be God, that attempts to take over and lets us play god ourselves. It's our human desire to live for ourselves without any responsibility to God or to anyone else. The Bible calls that rebellion against God *sin*.

As I write these words, the United States is reverberating with the aftershocks of the collapse of Enron, one of the biggest bankruptcies in American history. One former executive of the company was found dead of an apparent suicide. Thousands of people have seen their investment nest eggs fall from the wall and crash to the ground. Their lives have been disrupted and their trust shattered. Many of these lives will never be put back together again. Congressional hearings have been called. The political fault lines are beginning to emerge. It's too early to see all of the ways that Enron has affected the life of our nation. One industry analyst sounded like an Old Testament prophet when he said, "The woods were filled with smart people at Enron, but there were really no wise people, or people who could say, 'This is enough.'" He described the obsession with profits at Enron like a cancer that was set to metastasize (*The New York Times,* January 13, 2002, National section; page 26).

The biblical writers would understand what happened at Enron. It is a dramatic illustration of the destructive energy of unmitigated greed and arrogant power. The root of the problem at Enron was sin. The Bible says that, in an almost infinite variety of forms, that same sinful lust for power infects every one of us. In his classic interpretation of the Christian faith entitled *Mere Christianity* (Touchstone, 1996), C. S. Lewis described our dilemma. (The generic use of the word *man* reflects the era in which Lewis wrote, but it does not diminish the accuracy of his words.)

> Now what was the sort of "hole" man had got himself into? He had tried to set up on his own, to behave as if he belonged to himself. In other words, fallen man is not simply an imperfect creature who needs improvement: he is a rebel who must lay down his arms. (page 59)

There's an old story about the day Calvin Coolidge, who was noted for being a man of very few words, came home from church. His wife asked, "What did the preacher talk about?" The soft-spoken President said, "Sin." "Well," she asked, "what did he have to say about it?" Coolidge said, "He's against it."

And so is God. The creative God who first looked out on creation and said, "That's good!" is eternally opposed to anything that destroys or demeans the goodness of the creation. To affirm that God is "holy" is to declare that the God who breathed into human beings the breath of life, is unalterably opposed to anything that destroys or cheapens or abuses that life. All the power of an infinitely loving God is bound and determined to do everything that God can do to put things back together again, to renew this broken creation, to heal our broken lives, and to restore the harmony and wholeness that God always intended.

Eugene O'Neill is generally recognized as one of America's greatest dramatists. He often wrestled with deeply spiritual issues. In the closing scene of his play *The Great God Brown*, his main character says, "Life is imperfect, Brothers! Men have their faults, Sister! But with a few drops of glue much may be done! . . . This is Daddy's bedtime secret for today: Man is born broken. He lives by mending. The grace of God is glue!" (*The Plays of Eugene O'Neill*; New York: Random House, 1954; page 318). *Grace*—the utterly unmerited, undeserved, unearned love of God—is the glue by which God is at work to put things back together again.

Paul uses a powerful word to describe the way God is putting things back together. The word is *reconcile* or *reconciliation*. It literally means to bring things that have been separated back together again, to settle a dispute, to bring things into agreement and harmony. Here's the way he describes it in the second letter to the church at Corinth:

> For the love of Christ urges us on, because we are convinced that one has died for all; therefore all have died. And he died for all, so that those who live might live no longer for themselves, but for him who died and was raised for them.
>
> From now on, therefore, we regard no one from a human point of view; even though we once knew Christ from a human point of view, we know him no longer in that way. So if anyone is in Christ, there is a new creation: everything old has passed away; see, everything has become new! All this is from God, who reconciled us to himself through Christ, and has given us the ministry of reconciliation; that is, in Christ God was reconciling the world to himself, not counting their trespasses against them, and

entrusting the message of reconciliation to us. So we are ambassadors for Christ, since God is making his appeal through us; we entreat you on behalf of Christ, be reconciled to God. For our sake he made him to be sin who knew no sin, so that in him we might become the righteousness of God.

(2 Corinthians 5:14-21)

Did you notice who is doing the work of reconciliation? Paul says that "all this is from God." There is no doubt in the apostle's mind that God is the subject of the active verb. God is the one who took the initiative in the movement toward reconciliation. It's not sinful humanity who moved toward God, but God who moved toward us. God has done for us that which we could never do for ourselves in Christ. God has acted to reconcile us, to bring us back into harmony with God's life and purpose. The only hope for putting things back together again is the reconciling love that God has revealed at the cross.

Did you notice how God goes about the work of reconciliation? In his letter to the Colossians, Paul writes, "You who were once estranged and hostile in mind, doing evil deeds, he has now reconciled in his fleshly body through death, so as to present you holy and blameless and irreproachable before him" (Colossians 1:21-22). God has taken our rebellion, our sin, the brokenness of our lives to death on the cross. God overcomes our rebellion by the sacrifice of his own Son.

Did you notice what is included in God's reconciliation? "Through him God was pleased to reconcile to himself all things, whether on earth or in heaven, by making peace through the blood of his cross" (Colossians 1:20). God's reconciling love at the cross is not just for human beings in their relationship with God but also for human beings in relationship with one another and for all of the broken structures of our sin-shattered world. God does not settle for merely putting things back together the way they were before the Fall. Instead, God puts together a whole new creation, with a new way of living and thinking and acting and being that is filled with nothing less than the Resurrection power of the living Christ.

And did you notice the task to which God calls every follower

of Jesus Christ? God "has given us the ministry of reconciliation" (2 Corinthians 5:18). God has entrusted the work of reconciliation to every one of us. "We are ambassadors for Christ,
since God is making his appeal through us" (2 Corinthians
5:20). Every person whose broken life has been put back
together by the love of God at the cross is called to be about the
business of putting the broken pieces of this world back
together by the power of that same self-giving love.

One of those "ambassadors for Christ" who is helping put
things back together is Desmond Tutu, recipient of the Nobel
Peace Prize, retired archbishop of Cape Town, and the spiritual
leader of the movement for freedom and justice that brought an
end to apartheid and gave birth to the new South Africa. Anyone
who has heard him speak will remember the boundless energy,
unbridled joy, and undefeatable hope of this disciple of Christ.

His most recent act of ministry was in leading the Truth and
Reconciliation Commission. It demonstrated for the entire
world a radically different way of dealing with the painful truth
of South Africa's history in a way that brought the hope of healing and reconciliation for the future. One of the foundational
elements in the work of the Commission was defined in the
African word *ubuntu*. The word is notoriously difficult to trans-
late into English, in part because it represents a vision of
human life that is radically different from the individualized
assumptions of European and American culture. *Ubuntu*, as
Archbishop Tutu writes, defines "the very essence of being
human. . . . My humanity is caught up, is inextricably bound
up, in yours. . . . A person is a person through other persons"
(*No Future Without Forgiveness;* New York: Doubleday, 1999;
page 31). This understanding of human identity merged with
Christian theology in the assurance that "ultimately no one is an
irredeemable cause devoid of all hope. . . . God does not give up
on anyone, for God loved us from all eternity, God loves us now
and God will always love us, all of us good and bad, forever and
ever" (Tutu, page 85). Archbishop Tutu led both the resistance to
apartheid and the reconciliation with apartheid's enforcers in the
confidence that "this is a moral universe, which means that,
despite all the evidence that seems to be to the contrary, there

is no way that evil and injustice and oppression and lies can have the last word. . . . During the dark days of the struggle, when the morale of our people was often low in the face of rampant evil, I used to say: 'This is a moral universe—the upholders of apartheid have already lost.' I also used to appeal to our white fellow South African:'. . . Join the winning side'" (Tutu, pages 86–7).

Having experienced the good news of God's reconciliation, it's no wonder that Paul lived with a burning urgency to offer new life in Christ to every creature. As Christ's ambassador, he offered the bold invitation, "Be reconciled to God." He offers the same invitation to us. Allow your life to be swept up in the renewing, restoring, and reconciling love of God at the cross and become the agent of that same reconciliation in this severely broken and infinitely loved world.

Questions for Discussion and Reflection

1. Where do you see the evidence of brokenness in our world? in your life?

2. What is your understanding of "the Fall" (see Genesis Chapters 1–3 for background) and "sin"? How have you experienced them?

3. Where have you seen or experienced the grace of God as the "glue" that puts things together? What evidence do you see of God's work of reconciliation in your life? in our world?

4. What would it mean for you to "lay down your arms" and surrender to the reconciling love of God at work in your life? How could you become an ambassador for Christ's reconciliation?

Prayer

Reconciling God, meet us in all our brokenness, and by your grace put the shattered pieces of our lives back together again. Then, by your Spirit, make us the agents of your reconciling love in this broken world. Amen.

Holy Week

Why Did Jesus Die on the Cross?
To Set Us Free:
Leave Your Chains Behind

Mark 10:42-45; Romans 7:14–8:17

C*hains.* There is, I suspect, no stronger symbol of slavery than the chains.

While I was working on this study, the nation celebrated the twenty-fifth anniversary of Alex Haley's landmark historical novel, *Roots.* It hardly seemed possible that a quarter of a century had passed since its publication. I remember reading most of the book during some cold, gray winter days when the weather conspired with the story to take me into a deep, dark place in my soul. The book and the subsequent television miniseries had the same impact on America in the late twentieth century as *Uncle Tom's Cabin* had the century before; both exposed to plain view the brutal horror of slavery in America.

We caught another glimpse of it in Stephen Spielberg's powerful movie *Amistad.* It tells the story of the 1839 revolt by fifty-three Africans who rebelled against their captors on the Spanish slave ship *La Amistad* and of the New England abolitionists who fought for their freedom. At several points throughout the movie, Spielberg uses the sound of the clanking chains to draw our emotions into the injustice they represent.

The case of the prisoners from *La Amistad* went all the way to the US Supreme Court, where former President John Quincy

Adams argued for and finally helped to secure their freedom. In the film, retired Supreme Court Justice Harry Blackmun played the part of the justice who read the final verdict. Justice Blackmun's daughter wrote that "after 34 years of public service, championing the rights of . . . anyone . . . who has been stomped down, it seems appropriate that my father has made his last public appearance on the Big Screen [serving that cause]" (*The Orlando Sentinel, Florida Magazine,* January 18, 1998; page 14). Having known Justice Blackmun personally, I knew that his final public act was a witness to his life-long commitment to the liberating power of the love of God in Christ. It pointed toward part of the story that doesn't appear in the movie. Because of the witness and support of the Christian abolitionists who fought for them, many of those prisoners became Christians. When they returned to Africa, they planted the church in their native land.

Though few of us could ever know or understand the full horror of human slavery, and though all of us continue to struggle with its corrosive effects in the bloodstream of our nation's history, the Bible says that in a spiritual sense, we've all been in chains. The Bible says that every last one of us, along with this whole damaged creation, has been in slavery to sin and death. I wonder what form those spiritual chains take in *your* life.

Some of us are in bondage to the all-consuming passions of a damaged ego that continues to demand more and more attention for itself with no regard to God or anyone else.

Some of us are imprisoned by greed, social status, pride, or bigotry.

Some of us are bound by damaged emotions and painful memories from the past.

Some of us are imprisoned in self-destructive addictions to drugs, alcohol, or sex.

Some of us know that we have been called to a better life, born for a higher purpose, destined for a greater calling; but we continue to be dragged down by old habits, old fears, and old attitudes that hold us back from the life we know we were created to live.

Some of us are enslaved by fear of our own mortality and the awesome power of death.

The list could go on, but the Bible says that all of us have been in chains. We all experience slavery to sin and death. In the seventh chapter of his letter to Rome, the apostle Paul described his own inner conflict with bondage and freedom. Eugene Peterson captures the feeling of the struggle in his contemporary paraphrase of the apostle's words:

> I know the law but still can't keep it, and if the power of sin within me keeps sabotaging my best intentions, I obviously need help! I realize that I don't have what it takes. I can will it, but I can't *do* it. I decide to do good, but I don't *really* do it; I decide not to do bad, but then I do it anyway. . . . The moment I decide to do good, sin is there to trip me up. . . . I've tried everything and nothing helps. I'm at the end of my rope. Is there no one who can do anything for me?   (Romans 7, selected verses, *Message*)

Paul can see the life for which he was created, but he is bound up in things that hold him back and weigh him down. I suspect that if we are ruthlessly honest with ourselves, we know how he felt. We have moments when we catch a glimpse of the whole, free person God intends for us to be; but something keeps us from experiencing the freedom that we know God intends.

Now and then we catch a glimpse of that kind of freedom in unexpected places. Mike Krzyzewski is the coach of the Duke University Blue Devils men's basketball team. He's been to nine Final Fours and seven national championship games. He was getting ready to play for the national championship again. Duke and Arizona were evenly matched. It was anyone's guess who would win. The pressure to win must have been overwhelming. But I found an amazing freedom in hearing him say, "Win or lose, I'll feel the same way about my team. I won't need beating Arizona to define how I feel about this year. When we went to all those Final Fours and won two national titles, you get into the thing of, 'You have to do that in order to be happy.' That's wrong. I'm going to be really happy if we win. If we lose, I'll be sad for that night. Whether I don't win a national championship again or I win four more, I'll be the same. I love what I do" (*The Tampa Tribune*, April 2, 2001).

I'd call that freedom. Freedom from the bondage of everyone else's expectations. Freedom to do the best you can do and let the consequences take care of themselves. Freedom from the need to defeat someone else to build yourself up. Coach K's words sounded like the words of a person who is internally free to face whatever comes. His words sounded something like that freedom that God intends for creation.

I felt the joy of that kind of freedom in a very bright, talented, engaging young man in my congregation. Shortly after coming to Tampa, he shared with me the story of his addiction to alcohol and drugs and of the way Alcoholics Anonymous has been the tool of God's liberation in his life. He helps lead a weekly AA celebration that brings over 100 people to our church. Recently he stopped me on Sunday morning, wrapped his arms around me, and told me that in the gathering the night before, he had celebrated twelve years of sobriety. He knows how it feels to be set free!

Having struggled with his own bondage in the seventh chapter of Romans, Paul comes barreling into the eighth chapter with the good news of God's freedom.

> There is therefore now no condemnation for those who are in Christ Jesus. For the law of the Spirit of life in Christ Jesus has set you free from the law of sin and of death. For God has done what the law, weakened by the flesh, could not do: by sending his own Son in the likeness of sinful flesh, and to deal with sin, he condemned sin in the flesh, so that the just requirement of the law might be fulfilled in us, who walk not according to the flesh but according to the Spirit. For those who live according to the flesh set their minds on the things of the flesh, but those who live according to the Spirit set their minds on the things of the Spirit. To set the mind on the flesh is death, but to set the mind on the Spirit is life and peace. (Romans 8:1-6)

Across these weeks of Lent, we've been asking the question: Why did Jesus die on the cross? As we follow the track that leads through the events of Holy Week, even with the waving of palm branches and the shouts of "Hosanna!" in the air, we can see more clearly than ever before the dark shadows of Good Friday looming out ahead of us. There is no turning back now. This week's pathway will take us to the cross. The answer we hear from the apostle this week is that Jesus died to set us free. Jesus went to the cross to liberate us from slavery to sin and death. Jesus died to set us free from the things that hold us down and keep us back from becoming the whole, joyful, free people that God intended for us to be. Jesus died to set you free.

A third-century theologian named Origen spoke of the "ransom" theory of the atonement. It was rooted in Jesus' word to his disciples that "the Son of Man came not to be served but to serve, and to give his life a ransom for many" (Matthew 20:28). Across the centuries, theologians have tended to ask some very difficult questions about this interpretation. How does Jesus' death pay the ransom for my sin? Who required the payment? To whom was the ransom paid? These are, I guess, good questions for scholars to ask. But I'm fairly well convinced that they are utterly irrelevant for people who know how it feels to be in chains and who have found in the self-giving love of the cross the power of God to set them free. The critical factor is not *how* it happens, but *that* it happens in the real experience of people like you and me.

In *Mere Christianity*, C. S. Lewis makes a critically important distinction between the reality of the Christian faith and our attempted explanations of it.

> Theories about Christ's death are not Christianity: they are explanations about how it works. . . . [T]he thing itself is infinitely more important than any explanations that theologians have produced. . . . We are told that Christ was killed for us, that His death has washed out our sins, and that by dying He disabled death itself. That is the formula. That is Christianity. That is what has to be believed.   (pages 58–9)

How do we experience the reality of this understanding of the atonement? Imagine for a moment that you were a slave, standing on the auction block, in chains. Imagine that the price hanging over your head is astronomically beyond anything that you would ever be able to pay to buy your freedom. Imagine that someone stepped up to the auction block and offered to pay the price to set you free. Imagine that your liberator paid the price by taking your place. Imagine that somehow the self-offering of that single liberator ended the whole institution of slavery. And imagine how it would feel to walk away from that auction block as one who had been set free! Now, name the specific chains that bind you, and surrender them to the power of God's liberating love revealed at the cross.

Malcolm Muggeridge was a leading editorial writer in Great Britain, writing for the *Manchester Guardian* and editing a satirical magazine called *Punch*. Then he became a Christian. Here's the way he described the freedom he found in Christ.

> This is freedom—the sense of belonging to God's creation; these are our human rights—to participate in the realization of [God's] purposes for it.
>
> It is like coming to after an anaesthetic; reconnecting with reality after being enmeshed in fantasy. . . . I find myself imprisoned in the tiny dungeon of my ego, fettered and bound hand and foot with the appetites of the flesh and the will, unable to move or to see. Then I notice that light is somehow filtering in, and I become aware that there is a window through which I can look out. Looking out, I see the vast expanses of eternity bathed in the light of God's universal love. The window focuses this light as the Incarnation focused God's love, thereby miraculously bringing it within the dimensions of time, and procuring my release. My bonds and fetters fall away; I break out of the tiny dungeon of my ego like a butterfly out of its chrysalis. I am free.
>
> ("The Fearful Symmetry of Freedom," *Christianity Today,*
> April 21, 1978; page 15)

The good news for every enslaved one of us is that because of what Christ has done for us at the cross, we can leave our chains behind. As we allow the love of God in Christ to break into the bondage of our lives, we can be set free to rise up and follow Jesus in the way that leads to the new life of the

Resurrection. The explanations are sure to be inadequate, but the reality can change our lives!

Questions for Discussion and Reflection

1. What are the chains that bind you today? What is keeping you from being the whole, free person God created you to be?

2. Read Romans 7:14-24. What do you hear Paul saying in this passage? How can you identify with the spiritual struggle he describes?

3. Read Romans 8:1-4, 10-11. How have you experienced the kind of freedom the apostle proclaims in these verses? Can you identify the freedom described in this chapter by Malcolm Muggeridge?

4. What new understanding or insight has this chapter brought to you regarding Jesus' selfless act in giving us freedom?

Prayer

Liberating God, by your self-giving love, set us free from our bondage that we might follow you in the way that leads to new life. Amen.

Good Friday

Why Did Jesus Die on the Cross? To Accomplish Our Salvation: It Is Finished!

John 19:17-30

ood Friday is the place where the track gave out. It is the one single, decisive spot in the struggle between good and evil, love and hate, God's mercy and our sin. There is no way to outflank or avoid it. It was the only place where the final battle could be joined. In John's Gospel, the last thing we hear at the cross is Jesus' dying cry, "It is finished."

There are, of course, two ways in which those words could be said. *It is finished* could mean "It's over. Done. Kaput." The words could contain the dismal sorrow of a failed political campaign. You've heard the defeated candidates' speeches. You've seen them gather with their weary family around the microphone. You've watched them attempt to keep a stiff upper lip as they look out at their weeping supporters. "Thank you for your support. You've been a great team. We did the best we could, but the votes are in, and it went the other way. It's time to fold up the chairs, throw away the posters, and go back to life the way it was before. It's been great, but it's over and done. It is finished."

And, to tell you the truth, that's the way Jesus' story should have ended. By all the human evidence, that's exactly what we have here. Look at him up there, nailed to that Roman cross.

Jesus is defeated by his opposition, abandoned by his friends, rejected by the crowds who voted for Barabbas's survival over that of Jesus, mocked by the soldiers who nailed him to the cross to prove again the victory of the loveless power of the sword over the powerless love of the spirit. By every human standard, Jesus was finished, kaput, over and out. He had lost the battle with the power of evil.

That's what it should have been—but that's not the way it turned out. We know, as radio commentator Paul Harvey would say, "the rest of the story." We know that when the world was finished with Jesus, God wasn't finished with his work of redemption and grace. We know that when Jesus said, "It is finished," he meant, "It is completed!" The task was done. The mission was accomplished. The purpose for which Jesus came among us was fulfilled. We dare to believe that at this moment in history, when Jesus bowed his head and gave up his spirit, God had done everything that needed to be done for the salvation of the world. This is everything the love of God could do to save us, and it's all that we need. At the cross of Jesus, God's love had done everything that needed to be done to save every one of us and to redeem the whole groaning creation. This is what it cost God to save us.

Interestingly enough, two of the biggest movies in Hollywood history have spoken to what it means to be saved. One is Steven Spielberg's blockbuster *Saving Private Ryan*. It begins on D-Day, World War II, with what many veterans say is the most accurate depiction of the invasion of Normandy that has ever been made. It conveys the brutal, bloody reality of the price that was paid in the invasion that determined the outcome of the war. There would still be many struggles ahead, but after D-Day, there was no doubt about who would ultimately win. In the same way, the cross of Christ marked the ultimate invasion of saving love into this broken and brutal world. There are still struggles ahead, but to hear Jesus say, "It is finished," is to know that ultimately the love of God revealed at the cross is the only thing that can save this world and each of us in it from self-destruction.

The second blockbuster movie was James Cameron's *Titanic*.

In spite of some of the movie's syrupy teenage-romance excess, it touches some of the deep emotions that continue to surround one of the defining moments of the twentieth century. All of the arrogant optimism of human wisdom and technology sinks into watery darkness because of a rip in the hull of the ship. In the movie, the aged Rose looks back on that tragic night, with all its suffering and death, and she says of her love, Jack, in effect, "He saved me in every way one person can save another."

To hear Jesus cry, "It is finished," is to know that the love of God revealed in Jesus has saved us in every way we could ever hope to be saved. Of course, there is a difference. When Rose said it of Jack, it was fiction. When we say it of Jesus, it is for real.

Questions for Reflection and Discussion

1. Talk about a time in your life when you have experienced a saving love. How were you changed by this love?

2. Where did you first hear the story of Jesus' death on the cross? What is your earliest or most vibrant memory of Good Friday?

3. Read through or reflect back upon the Passion story in John, chapters 18 and 19. What moment in the story touches you most deeply, and in what way?

4. Reflect upon and share the feelings you have when you hear Jesus say, "It is finished." Spend some quiet time on your own reflecting upon the passion and death of Jesus. Allow the death of Jesus to soak into your soul.

Prayer

O God, it is finished. You have done everything that Infinite Love could do to save us. May we, O God, do everything we can to live within that saving love. Amen.

Easter

Why Did Jesus Die on the Cross? To Defeat Death: Victory in the Graveyard

Luke 24:1-9; 1 Corinthians 15

The only place to begin on Easter Sunday morning is the place where all of our stories end. Luke says, "On the first day of the week, at early dawn, they came to the tomb" (24:1). The only place to begin is in a graveyard. It's the place where our track runs out, the final stop on every human journey.

Magrey deVega serves with me in the pastoral leadership of Hyde Park United Methodist Church. He came to us from Bethel United Methodist Church in Tallahassee, Florida. One of the oldest congregations in our state, Bethel has been there for 168 years. Like most old, rural, southern churches, it has its own cemetery. But the cemetery is so old that if there ever was a plan for the arrangement of the graves, it was forgotten long ago. Magrey said that there are gravestones scattered all over the property. Unsuspecting folks will park their car and discover that they've just driven over a grave. The picnic tables where the congregation gathers for "dinner on the grounds" are set amid gravestones. The church is literally surrounded by graves.

When Magrey described the Bethel cemetery to us, I could not help but think that it was a very practical image of the way the church lives its life and proclaims its faith in a world that is simply cluttered with death. Death is all around us. We face it at every turn. Sometimes it comes as a peaceful release at the end of long suffering. Often it comes as a brutal interruption of the ongoing flow of life. However and whenever it comes, death is all around us. Try as we might, we cannot escape it.

So, the women "came to the tomb, taking the spices that they had prepared" (Luke 24:1). I love these women. They always remind me of the women in the movie *Steel Magnolias*. They were no-nonsense, down-to-earth realists. They had stuck with Jesus to the bitter, gruesome end. They had watched Jesus die. They had seen his broken body taken down from the cross. And now, they had followed the sad procession to the tomb, on the property of Joseph of Arimathea. They saw the place where the body was laid. They knew death when they saw it, and they knew what to do. With their embalming spices in hand, they were on their way to finish their work, to perform this last human act of love for the one they called Master and Lord. In coming to the tomb, they ultimately would become the best known—not to mention the most surprised—morticians in history!

The story begins where all our stories end, and if we are to experience its power, that's where we have to begin too. We begin with the awesome reality of death. There's no use trying to deny, evade, or avoid it. There's no way to camouflage it with lilies or drown it out with choral "alleluias." Martin Marty said we might as well talk about death, because there sure is a lot of it going around these days. The grave is the end of the track. Humanly speaking, this is where the rails give out.

There are times, of course, when death comes almost as a friend at the conclusion of a long and useful life or, as mentioned earlier, as the peaceful conclusion to a time of suffering. One Holy Saturday, the silent day that Jesus' body lay in the tomb, I visited with a woman who, if she were not dying, would soon be 105 years old. She was under hospice care and was actively engaged in the process of dying. After the visit, her son said to me, "We don't look on this as a tragedy. We see it as a promise fulfilled." There is a time when it's OK to die.

But even when death is on its best behavior, we still know that it is the ultimate contradiction of life, the ruthless opponent of the creative, life-giving purpose of God. The apostle Paul got it right when he called death "the last enemy" (1 Corinthians 15:26).

During Holy Week in 2001, I listened to the attorney general and the head of the Bureau of Prisons analytically outline the process by which our government planned to put convicted US terrorist Timothy McVeigh to death. I heard their hope that McVeigh's execution would bring "closure" for the families of the victims of his horrific crime. That's the word they used, *closure*—like the closure of dirt in the grave, like the heavy thud of a huge stone being rolled over the entrance to the tomb.

As I listened, I realized that closure is just about all this death-cluttered world has to give. When it comes down to the end, all our human powers can do is close the story with the heavy thud of death. As I listened to them talk about putting McVeigh to death, something deep within me wanted to shout back at the screen, Isn't there something within us that cries out for *more* than the closure of death? Isn't there something of the Spirit of God within us that longs for every broken heart to be mended, for every promise to be fulfilled, and for death in all of its forms to be defeated? Isn't there something deeper than vengeance within us that hopes for death to be overcome by new life?

Whenever and wherever you are right now, I'm confident that reruns of *M*A*S*H* are being shown on some cable channel. In one of my favorite episodes, Captain Benjamin "Hawkeye" Pierce was performing a rather ordinary piece of surgery. The doctors were bantering back and forth as they usually do. Suddenly, Margaret, the serious-minded nurse, shouted, "I've lost his pulse!" Immediately all the energy in the operating room was focused on saving that patient's life. Hawkeye pounded on the soldier's chest and shouted, "Hang on, kid! don't let that b——— [death] win!" He opened the soldier's chest and began massaging his heart. Finally, Margaret said, "I have a pulse." Exhausted, Hawkeye fell back from the table to catch his breath.

There was a reporter in the operating room that day. He was amazed at what he had just seen. Later, when he asked Colonel

Potter about it, Potter, in his always fatherly and understanding way, said, "You have to understand that when it comes to death, Pierce is a very sore loser." And so is God!

The women went to the tomb that morning expecting nothing more than the kind of "closure" this death-weary world had conditioned them to expect. But what they found was the radical reversal of everything they expected. Luke records, "They found the stone rolled away from the tomb, but when they went in, they did not find the body" (24:2-3). And right there, in the very place where the only thing they had any right to expect was death, they heard the greatest question this gravestone-cluttered world has ever heard: "Why do you look for the living among the dead? He is not here, but has risen" (verse 5).

The story that begins with death ends with life. The story that begins in the closure of the tomb opens the door to eternity. The story that begins where all of our stories end, ends where our new life begins. The good news that the church announces on Easter morning is *not* that God has somehow brought closure to our human story and has somehow reconciled the world with death. The good news is that God has acted in the resurrection of Jesus Christ to overcome death with new life. I received an Internet Easter greeting from a preacher friend in Indiana the week after Easter. The message was, "Easter means that tomorrow is not just another day." The good news of the Resurrection is that our stories do not end in death. Tomorrow—along with all the tomorrows that lie before us—is never just another day. Christ is risen, and he goes before us through life into life everlasting.

Across these weeks of Lent we've been thinking about the question, Why did Jesus die on the cross? We've explored some of the biblical answers to that question. With Christians throughout the ages, we've searched for words and ideas with which to explain or convey the meaning of the cross. We've said that Jesus died to redeem the whole creation, to cleanse us from sin, to show us the way to live, to reconcile us to God and to one another, and to set us free. But all of it has been a prelude to the great good news of Easter morning. At the end of the track, Jesus died to win the victory over death. He died to give us the hope of eternal life. Paul declared it in his great *tour de force* on the Resurrection in 1 Corinthians 15:

> But in fact Christ has been raised from the dead, the first fruits of those who have died. For since death came through a human being, the resurrection of the dead has also come through a human being; for as all die in Adam, so all will be made alive in Christ. But each in his own order: Christ the first fruits, then at his coming those who belong to Christ. Then comes the end, when he hands over the kingdom to God the Father, after he has destroyed every ruler and every authority and power. For he must reign until he has put all his enemies under his feet. The last enemy to be destroyed is death. (verses 20-26)

The place where our human stories end is precisely the place where God's new life begins. The place where all of our human energies fail is the place where God wins the victory over death.

I've been proclaiming the Easter gospel as a pastor for nearly three decades. Every church I've served decorates the altar with lilies, many of which are given in memory of family and friends who have died. Each year I recognize many of the names on the memorial list. I was with some of them when they died. For some, I led the pallbearers to the cemetery with their casket. For some, I spoke the words that committed their body to the grave. I can tell you where their human stories ended. I can show you the place where their bodies were laid. But by the power of the risen Christ, I also know that the grave was not the end of their story. I know that by faith in Christ, the same power that raised Jesus from the dead has raised them to new life, and that they are more alive today than they ever were before.

Early in my ministry I learned a great lesson from a woman in Adel, Georgia. I had been invited to preach a revival at the First United Methodist Church in Adel. I was a young, green preacher. I must have been the last name on their list of preachers! But I had a wonderful time with those folks.

The first day I was there, the pastor took me to visit a woman who had been suffering with cancer in one of its most painful, most excruciating forms. I suspect she was not yet sixty years old. She had been through all the treatments. Everyone knew it was just a matter of time now until the end of her struggle. Just as we were preparing to leave, I asked her, "What have you learned through all of this?" I really wasn't ready for her answer. I expected her to say something about the love of her family or the support of her friends. I was surprised to see a sparkle come into those eyes that had been weary and dim. A huge smile spread across her face, and with great confidence, she said, "Just one thing: Jesus is Lord." The way she declared it left no doubt in my mind that this one affirmation contained all the strength with which she had faced her suffering and all of the hope with which she anticipated her death.

I heard about a widow who said she got tired of people saying to her they were sorry she had "lost" her husband. She said, "I haven't lost him. I know right where he is. He is alive in the presence of the risen Christ." I can't explain it to you. It's all a mystery to me. But that is, after all, exactly the way Paul described it:

> Listen, I will tell you a mystery! We will not all die, but we will all be changed, in a moment, in the twinkling of an eye, at the last trumpet. For the trumpet will sound, and the dead will be raised imperishable, and we will be changed. For this perishable body must put on imperishability, and this mortal body must put on immortality. When this perishable body puts on imperishability, and this mortal body puts on immortality, then the saying that is written will be fulfilled:
> "Death has been swallowed up in victory."
> "Where, O death, is your victory?
> Where, O death, is your sting?"
> The sting of death is sin, and the power of sin is the law. But thanks be to God, who gives us the victory through our Lord Jesus Christ. (1 Corinthians 15:51-57)

Robert Griffin, better known as "Griff" to his students, was the long-time chaplain at Notre Dame. He died of cancer, but he lived with a joyful confidence in the Resurrection. He once said, "Death is a bully whose nose should be tweaked, and I hope to be one of the tweakers. . . . I want to be present at resurrections that defeat death's victories . . . I want to greet death, when he comes irresistibly, with insolence and swagger, as though I were a baggy-pants clown to whom the final snickers belong" (*Notre Dame Magazine,* Winter 1999-2000, quoted in *Context,* June 1, 2000; page 6).

The "Harry Potter" phenomenon and the movie version of *The Lord of the Rings* helped to create a burst of interest in fantasy stories. My favorite set of children's stories is *The Chronicles of Narnia,* by C. S. Lewis. If I had my way, every parent would be required to read them out loud to their children before they get to third grade. It would do the parents a lot of good! The Christ figure in Lewis's tales is Aslan, the lion. The title of the final book in the series is *The Last Battle.* Here's what Lewis wrote on the last page:

> "There *was* a real railway accident," said Aslan softly. "Your father and mother and all of you are—as you used to call it in the Shadow-Lands—dead. The [school] term is over: the holidays have begun. The dream is ended: this is the morning." . . .
>
> [T]he things that began to happen after that were so great and beautiful that I cannot write them. And for us this is the end of all the stories, and we can most truly say that they all lived happily ever after. But for them it was only the beginning of the real story. All their life in this world . . . had only been the cover and the title page: now at last they were beginning Chapter One of the Great Story, which no one on earth has read: which goes on forever: in which every chapter is better than the one before.
>
> (Collier, 1970; pages 183–84)

The story, the *real* story, begins in the graveyard, where all our human stories end. It is there that we hear the good news, "He is not here! He is risen!" Thanks be to God who gives us the victory through our Lord Jesus Christ!

Questions for Discussion and Reflection

1. What is your most recent experience with death? Remembering that experience, in what ways can you identify with the women who went to the tomb?

2. What is your understanding of the word *closure?* How do you feel about the way it is interpreted in this chapter?

3. Read 1 Corinthians 15:12-28, 50-57 aloud, the way it might have been read to the congregation in Corinth. How does it make you feel about the reality of death?

4. What difference does the hope of the Resurrection make in the way you live your life today?

Prayer

O God, who raised Jesus Christ to new life, meet us at the place where all of our stories end, and by your power, transform them into the place where new life begins. Amen.